RIVERSIDE REMEMBERED

the Medway from

Chatham Intra to Lower Rainham

written and illustrated

by

John K.Austin

edited by

Rosemary Dellar

For my Granddaughter, Gemma Austin

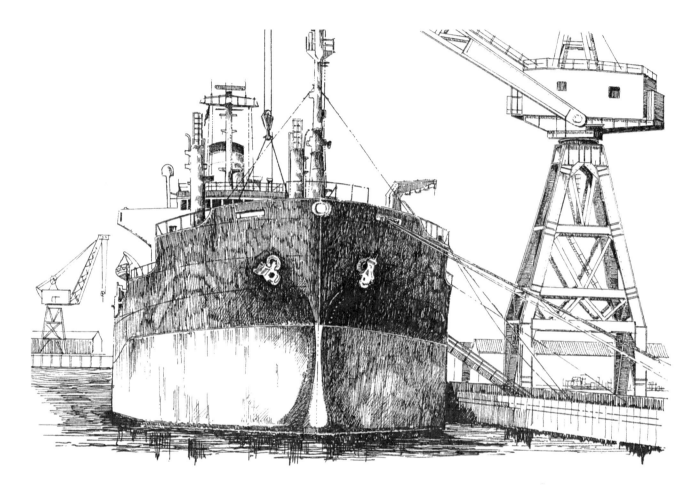

Chatham Maritime

Acknowledgments

Once more I must express my thanks to the many people who have helped in the preparation of this book - those who allowed me to wander on their land and sketch their property; others who volunteered information and answered my questions; and finally editor Rosemary Dellar and Betty Harrison of Minuteman Press who have brought the whole project to fruition.

Preface

My love of the river goes back to childhood days, when countless playtime hours were spent 'messing about on the river' at places like Sharp's Green, Motney Hill (called Motley Hill then) and other lonely stretches of the river bank in the vicinity of Lower Rainham. At that time there were many hulked remains of barges, forming, as they still do, marvellous things to play on. When I was sketching the *Lord Churchill* at Whitewall Creek there were some boys playing about on some of the old hulks still just visible in the slimy mud. Happy days!

At eleven years of age I joined the Scouts at Rainham, but two years later I swapped the shorts and woggle for bell-bottoms and enrolled as a member of the Gillingham Sea Cadets. On Saturdays, dressed in uniform, we would take the helm of one of Her Majesty's 'trot' boats as part of our navigation and seamanship training. Under instruction, threading our small boat past row upon row of anchored battleships and destroyers, we made for Sheerness, sometimes bringing back to Gillingham Pier ratings lucky enough to have a weekend pass. On Sundays we would sail our whalers off the Strand in competition with the *Arethusa* boys, but they always won. We would also spend hours scraping the bottoms of our boats in Chatham Dockyard, in between crafty puffs from a packet of Woodbines.

Later, as an impoverished art student, I found a holiday job as third hand on the sailing barge *Greta* with Skipper Tom Dennis, whose vast knowledge of the Thames and Medway - their tides, sandbanks, buoys, creeks, wharves and quays - was unbelievable. Underway in dense fog or in the middle of the night he would know exactly where we were just by a twitch of his weather-beaten nose.

Though my student days are long past, I still find drawing the scenes along the Medway shore as enjoyable as ever despite the dumping of rubbish which disfigures its banks at some points, and the deterioration which has taken place since the closure of many waterside industries. These were originally attracted to the river as an efficient means of transport, with raw materials easily available close by. But where factories have closed Nature has often done a splendid job in camouflaging the ugly remains, with many native plants gently waving in the Medway breeze, splashing an otherwise barren landscape with brilliant contrasting colours. It is my hope that my work will bring others to appreciate our waterside heritage and help to preserve it for future generations to enjoy.

John K. Austin

Editor's Note

Since John Austin completed his drawings and descriptive account of the shores of the Lower Medway in the late 1980s, enormous changes have occurred along its banks. The industries which once flourished there have almost all disappeared, to be replaced by new housing or leisure developments. Therefore the author's original text is presented unaltered to record the end of an era in the life of the River Medway. Two earlier books ('The Medway Shore as it was, from Burham to Borstal' and 'Yesterday's Medway from Rochester Bridge to Chatham Intra') told part of the story: this volume completes the set.

Rosemary Dellar.

FORT PITT

Before leaving Chatham Intra mention must be made of Fort Pitt, high above St Bartholomew's Hospital. Now the site is occupied by the maze of corridors, exhibition halls, studios and workshops that make up the new Art School building of the late sixties. This replaced the huge crater which was all that remained of the original Fort Pitt. Serving as a garrison for troops between 1810 and 1814, its bleakness had quite an impression on Dickens, who set the duel scene between Mr Winkle and Dr Slammer in `The Pickwick Papers' here. By the 1840s it had become a hospital for wounded soldiers, and after the Crimean War in 1854 additional hospital buildings were erected. Some of these now form part of Fort Pitt Grammar School for Girls, which commands some fine panoramic Medway views of Bridge Reach, Limehouse Reach and Chatham.

Florence Nightingale opened the first Army Medical School here in 1860, and Queen Victoria paid three visits to the hospital, which eventually closed in 1922.

Looking across Limehouse Reach from Frindsbury to Fort Pitt

KETTLE HARD AND LONDON WHARF (LIMEHOUSE REACH)

Kettle Hard is little bit of the Medway river bank which is hidden away, out of sight behind `Sir John Hawkins' Hospital for Aged and Infirm Chatham Mariners and Shipwrights'. This little square of tranquil and lovingly-kept terraced cottages was founded in 1592 and rebuilt in 1722. Set behind wrought iron railings on either side of a small chapel fronted by a well, it lies at the boundary between Chatham and Rochester.

The narrow passage beside it which leads towards the river invites the inquisitive to ignore the rubbish, including what must surely be the hallmark of the decade, a wheel-less shopping trolley, and emerge out of the gloom at the small but peaceful sheltered bay known in times past as Kettle Hard. Although local maps indicate the names of various wharves and quays in this area the odd name of `Kettle Hard' does not appear even in the 1897 survey. But the present Medway Ports Authority berthing chart for the Port of Rochester does mention Kettle Hard as yacht moorings. The name is also remembered with affection by the older generation with greying hair and a sound knowledge of yesterday's river. Ask any such, and they will tell you that Limehouse Reach has two hards, Bath Hard, between Furrell's Creek and Doust's Slipway (sometimes referred to as Gill's Cottages, not far from where the railway passes over the High Street), and Kettle Hard at the old boundary, next to London Wharf.

GPS Tugs at Limehouse Reach

The Thames lighter illustrated on the front cover, with its front and back entrances, actually straddles the boundary between Rochester and Chatham. On the Rochester side is the old `City Boundary Wharf', whose annual rent in 1861 was 1s.4d (approximately 7p). Further extensions were made in 1866 by Alfred Hanson, a name long associated with the retailing of domestic coal. On the Chatham side of the hard are the remains of the once well-known London Wharf, which, like so many others in this lower part of Limehouse Reach, belonged to a brewery. The owner in the 1890s was Jude Hanbury, whose company was at Wateringbury near Maidstone. Another well-known firm, Truman Hanbury Buxton, of the Black Eagle brewery in Spitalfields, also had a wharf close by which regularly berthed its sailing barge *Black Eagle* when she brought her twice-weekly cargo of beer. The large number of wharves associated with brewery firms is not unexpected, as the Ordnance Survey map of 1864 shows that there were twelve public houses between the Rochester boundary and the `Sun' hotel at the top of Medway Street. In contrast there were four places of worship in the same area.

Kettle Hard was once a sandy shingled bay, but now it is mostly mud. This was one of the places used by Medway fishermen in the nineteenth century to tend their boats and mend their nets while their offspring played happily on the sandy beach. This idyllic view of Kettle Hard is a long way from the reality of today, as illustrated by the somewhat bedraggled flotilla of houseboats and other craft that use the hard as a secure anchorage. That the beach could once be walked at low tide between Bath Hard and Holborn Wharf near Sun Pier, where the Bourne entered the Medway (now Medway Street), is revealed by my research. Young girls in service to George Gill would use that route to the market at Chatham several times a week.

The name `Kettle Hard' is probably connected with old orders and ordinances which determined what the Medway fishing fraternity did and did not do. Rules of the Medway fishery dating from about 1785 state that it was an offence to use any net called a Kettle Net, or to fish for, catch or take any fish commonly called a Kettle Fish. Kettle nets were in principle land fish traps set into the soft shingle at low tide on a series of upright poles in such a way that the opening was on the land side only. Shoals of fish finding themselves trapped would easily be caught by the net operators, who would simply wade out as the tide receded to scoop up the fish. Unlike modern angling kettle-netting was not a leisure pursuit: for many at the turn of the century it was their way of earning a bob or two. In places like Dungeness fifty per cent of the mackerel landed were caught by kettle-netting.

The lower end of Limehouse Reach towards the river's sweep into Chatham Reach is littered with the remains of several old wharves. Apart from Kettle Hard Yacht Moorings, the current Ports Authority berthing chart lists only Mid-Kent Wharf (disused), and Anchorage Wharf. However a Victorian map which I studied in Chatham Library lists the following for the same stretch of river: London Wharf, Borough Wharf, High Street Wharf, Sun Wharf (Coal Depot), Town Mills and Flour Wharf, Bessent's Wharf, and, lastly, Holborn Wharf at the far end of Medway Street. The Flour Wharf was later known as Scott's Wharf and Gammon's Wharf.

The converted M.T.B. shown in the illustration, with the smaller cabin launch tied up starboard side, is berthed at Empire Wharf - or so the hand-painted sign at the top of the gangway says. Empire Wharf, according to the old map, is where the High Street Wharf was. Perhaps the name was changed when the very popular Empire Theatre and Picture House graced the site. When I made the drawing the little garden was a mass of daffodils.

Moored vessels at Empire Wharf, Chatham

Sun Pier is no longer the river landmark it once was, since today it is minus its waiting rooms and ticket office surmounted with a clock and weathervane. These were particular features of the pier in the days of the Medway paddle steamers, when many local children would have considered their summer holidays incomplete without the annual trip to Sheerness, Margate or Southend. Unlike Ship Pier, which has an ancient past, Sun Pier dates back only to the 1830s, when a small jetty was erected at the site. During the construction of a much bigger pier in 1885 part of the newly-built pier gave way under the weight of the people waiting for the Upnor ferry, tipping many into the water. Fortunately no-one was killed, though some were injured. The pier was completed in 1886, then further enlarged a few years later.

In the early 1960s a serious fire raged through the pier's superstructure. Although it was fully restored at a cost of £85,000, being officially reopened in December 1987, the waiting rooms and ticket office were not replaced. Prior to the fire the ticket office had been used by the Ministry of Agriculture as an employment centre for land workers. Perhaps the only part of the old pier left at street level is the Pier Chambers building, whose little pointed turret suggests a fairy-tale stage backcloth.

On the corner of Medway Street and the High Street there once stood the `Sun' Hotel, a familiar landmark to many older people. The hotel was knocked down years ago, leaving an interesting gap which revealed old fireplaces, colourful scraps of wallpaper and old panelled doors. This soon became an eyesore, but now the entire corner site stretching right down to the river's edge at what is still Sun Wharf, and incorporating Pier Chambers, is a most pleasing and extremely well-designed complex. The paved public right-of-way along Sun Wharf from the pier, as seen in the drawing on page 7, is planned eventually to skirt the river and lead to Furrell's Creek.

It is difficult to determine the age of most of the older buildings, mainly shops, that back on to the river, because of the many facelifts and layers of camouflage painted and plastered on through decades of trading. When Grays, a name long associated with the High Street, pulled down their group of motorcycle shops the gap revealed the haphazard buildings and lean-to fabrications which had gradually extended the original accommodation. Patchwork views like this are normally hidden by the dovetailing of one building with the next, but a similar glimpse is possible a little further down the High Street where the old Empire Theatre was once joined to the `Von Alten' public house.

Where possible it is interesting to sneak round the back of these old riverside buildings. The rear area of the `Von Alten' is of particular architectural interest, especially the building next door to it. Many such structures tend to be covered by pebble-dash which hides their age, but the drawing shows three quite tall but extremely narrow brick buildings. One has the remnants of a sign painted on the brickwork which in Victorian days could be read by passing river traffic.

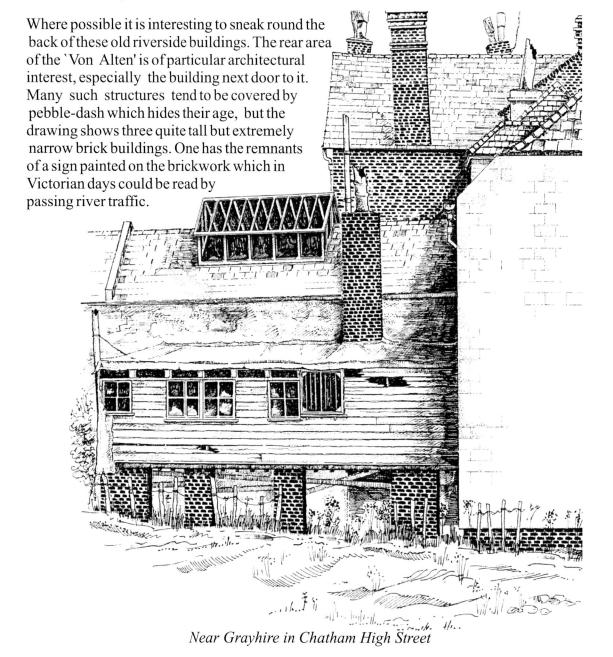

Near Grayhire in Chatham High Street

Rear of High Street Chatham, near Sun Wharf

Another public house which must be mentioned is the `King's Arms' along Medway Street. Legend has it that it was from a wharf at the rear of the ale-house which once stood on this site that Charles I made his escape to France after being heavily outnumbered by the opposing Cromwellians during the Civil War. It is quite possible, although in some history books the town of his departure is given as Brighton and not Chatham.

Gone from opposite the present public house is the terrace of neat Edwardian bay-fronted houses which once graced this street. Here the River Bourne flowed into the Medway from the hills around the town, giving its name to Holborn Wharf, which, according to Victorian maps, was the last wharf in Limehouse Reach. In the same vicinity was the shipyard of Sedger and Hogben, who built HMS *Assistance,* a warship of fifty guns, in 1747. Towards the end of the eighteenth century several other private shipyards followed, on both sides of Limehouse Reach, to meet the demands placed on the Navy by the war with France.

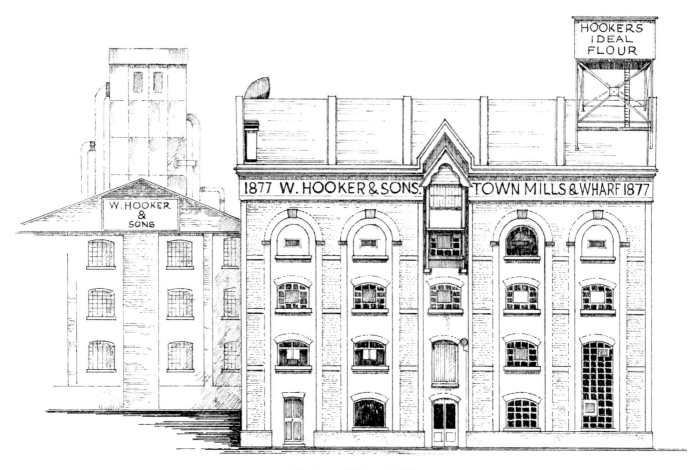

Hookers Flour Mill

Not only the old wharves have disappeared. Many old landmarks, like the Empire Theatre which had the Medway lapping almost at its foundations, and the Wingent and Kimmins flour warehouse, are now only memories. The former has been replaced by what Prince Charles might term a `carbuncle', for Anchorage House dwarfs its surrounding townscape. The Texas DIY warehouse has taken over the other site next to Sun Pier in Medway Street.

CHATHAM TOWN HALL, GUN WHARF, AND JILLINGHAM WATER

Close to the riverside in Chatham is the old Town Hall, designed in 1898 by George Best and built by West Brothers of Rochester. The site was originally a graveyard, and the tombstones of former residents of Chatham can still be seen near the boundary walls of the Town Hall Gardens. The Clock Tower, 130 feet in height and having seven floors within, was a well-known landmark for miles around until the Pentagon and Anchorage House were built. The statuette figures seen above the ornate facade of Portland stone represent Justice, Britannia, Agriculture and Music. Chatham's Town Hall was completed in January 1900, but today the administration of the Medway Towns (with the exception of Gillingham) is undertaken from the less imposing building, once Wingets, just across Rochester Bridge in Strood.

Remains of old cemetery, Rope Walk Gardens, Chatham

Perhaps Globe Lane took its name from the Royal Marine Garrison Theatre, built almost a mile away in Dock Road in 1879. I presume the Royal Marine cap badge, which features a globe surrounded by a laurel wreath, provided the name of the theatre, which was later taken over by Chatham Council. Lack of enthusiasm caused its failure: it closed in 1962 and was subsequently pulled down.

Buses, both the familiar green Maidstone and District vehicles and the green and brown Chatham Traction vehicles which had replaced the trams, waited on both sides of Military Road overlooking the Paddock. In late Victorian views of Chatham sheep are seen grazing in this area, which was once called `The Shrubbery'. Amid the trees was formerly the timber-clad Paddock Restaurant, which began humbly as the wartime Corporation Canteen. Between the Paddock, now pleasant gardens and flowerbeds, and the Riverside gardens lie the remains of Globe Lane. A decade or so ago the river was invisible from here because of the buildings on the west side. One of these was the `Old George', a Victorian public house remembered for its ornate mirrors and its pianola.

Gun Wharf and Mountbatten House

The size of Mountbatten House can be seen clearly in the illustration. It is the tallest building to grace the Medway skyline, and was completed in 1976 as part of the Pentagon shopping centre at a cost of over fourteen million pounds. (The Town Hall cost less than thirty thousand!) Behind the pleasing facade of Mountbatten House, with its frontage of slender buttresses of evenly-laid brick, are the shopping complex, multi-storey car park and central first-floor bus station. The entire project was an ambitious challenge, especially as this particular area of Chatham, `The Brook', was notorious for its flooding. The corner of Chatham it replaced housed several prominent businesses. Opposite the Town Hall Barnards, and, next door, Coopers, were both naval and military tailors known by every Chatham-based sailor from the Admiral to the lowest bell-bottomed rating. Other shops recalled in fading childhood memories are Ive and Low for pencils, paint and paper; Margerums, who were always open for sweets and a smoke, no matter what the hour; and Waltons, the surgical appliance shop, whose wares always amused us as boys. There were others too: the Working Men's Club, which was at one time, I believe, the `Welcome Institution for Soldiers and Seamen'; and Whittakers, another naval tailor. All is now history; thankfully the memory of this corner with its Senior Service connections will be kept alive by Mountbatten House, named after that great sailor Earl Mountbatten of Burma.

To the visitor there is nothing extra special about this bit of the Medway known as Gun Wharf, poised as it is on the river's bend between Limehouse and Chatham Reaches, below St Mary's Church, in the shadow of Mountbatten House and the Pentagon at Chatham. Now by courtesy of Lloyds a pleasant tree-lined walk skirts the river bank, although there is no sign or monument proclaiming that this stretch of the river, once simply `Jillingham Water', was once Henry VIII's winter anchorage on the Medway. Elizabeth I subsequently set up her royal dockyard here, with storehouse and a mast pond, on land between the church and the river. In the nineteenth century the cement and brick industries had brought prosperity, if only for a short while, to the small hamlets of the upper Medway beyond Rochester Bridge. Henry's policy of wintering some of his fleet in Jillingham Water, using the mud flats for graving the bottoms, had the same effect for a far longer period on the tiny lower riverside communities. These grew as the dockyard expanded, mushrooming into important naval and military towns.

Timber Store, Chatham Dockyard

As the name implies, Gun Wharf was where the guns and other armament from the warships moored in the Medway were stored or maintained. Although by the early nineteenth century the Dockyard was established further down the river opposite Upnor Castle, the gun wharf was still in use, as this graphic description in Brayley's `The Beauties of England and Wales' of 1808 shows:

`The Ordnance Wharf, which is not infrequently called the Old Dock, occupies a narrow slip of land below the chalk cliff between the church and the river. Here great quantities of naval ordnance are deposited in regular tiers, and abundance of cannonballs piled up in large pyramids. Great numbers of gun carriages are also laid up under cover, and in the store houses, and small armoury, are vast quantities of offensive weapons as pistols, cutlasses, pikes, poleaxes etc.'

Of the original Gun Wharf only the Command House, a very imposing riverside building, now a public house of the same name, remains. Built in 1758, in a period known as the `golden age' in domestic architecture, this fine example of the Georgian style illustrates its use of red brick, which with age has mellowed elegantly. Capped by a simple roof it was built to house the officer-in-charge of the Gun Wharf in the fashion appropriate to his rank and position. It stands near the giant stone groynes below St Mary's Church. Now the Heritage Centre, the church still stands sentinel above the river.

The Queens Harbourmaster's House, Chatham Dockyard

By 1799 more than two thousand workers were employed at the Dockyard, and from 1862 extensive expansion and modernisation took place. A new dock, then the largest in the world, was completed by 1900. Soon submarines were being built at Chatham, and the First World War brought much work building, repairing and refitting vessels of all kinds. The labour force dropped dramatically when that war ended, but rose again to 13,000 during World War II. But from then on closure was a growing threat, finally realised when John Nott announced to the House of Commons on 25th June 1981 that Chatham Dockyard was no longer viable.

This area of Chatham adjacent to the Gun Wharf has changed almost beyond recognition. Hopefully, what will never change is Chatham's link with the sea. The tall obelisk forming the war memorial to the Royal Navy was designed by Sir Robert Lorimer in 1924, with quadrant walls added by Sir Edward Maufe after World War II. It maintains the connection as it proclaims from the Great Lines high above Chatham the names of those who gave their lives not only for the town but for a free world extending far beyond the Medway.

Workshop, Chatham Dockyard

WHITEWALL CREEK AND CHATHAM NESS

The rotting disfigured remains of the once proud deep-sided wooden barge *Lord Churchill,* built by Harveys at Littlehampton, registered as a seventy-six ton ketch in 1888 and sole survivor of Walker and Howards' fleet of `Lords', are a sad reflection of her former glory. Converted to a `sprittie' by the Whitstable Shipping Company, she was finally used as a corn barge by Daniels Brothers of Whitstable. During her lifetime she was sunk and raised twice, first in Gravesend Reach in 1900, and again in 1933 at Becton. She was sold as a yacht in 1948, and eventually became a houseboat at Wouldham before ending her days at Whitewall Creek. Here the abandoned old-timer joined others in similar state in this watery graveyard, becoming an object for climbing by small boys in search of adventure.

Prior to the end of the last war the creek was used as a place where effluent was discharged by order of the Ministry of Supply. Previously in 1936 the dredging deposits from Limehouse and Bridge Reaches (79,287 tons of spoil) were dumped in the creek, in an early attempt to reclaim the tidal marsh forming this long spit of land. The muddy terrain affords one of the best views of the Medway Towns, with the former Naval Dockyard directly ahead across Chatham Reach. The area provided an ideal training ground for Chatham's Royal Marines to gain much-needed experience of tactical warfare at a time when Vls and V2s were falling from the skies.

It is hard to envisage the same place a hundred years earlier, when it boasted extensive brickfields owned by the Dean and Chapter of Rochester. There were two at Whitewall and another at Ten-Gun Field at Upnor. Brick making at this site had taken place since at least 1800. The importance of these brickfields can be assessed by the fact that at the height of production in the early 1840s one per cent of the nation's output of bricks came from Whitewall Creek. Nothing is left, nor does anything remain today of the cement works of Charles and James Formby, which occupied the area at the turn of the century. Gone too is the small wharf where once barges unloaded manure for local farmers.

There is no trace now, either, of the row of fourteen houses known as Whitewall Cottages. The end one, which was larger than the rest, was a public house called the `Shant', a gypsy word meaning `to drink'. It was owned by Budden and Biggs, whose slogan 'Body-building Beverages' was well-known at the time. At the back of the cottages was a small factory where fire bricks and round cobbles were manufactured.

There are three possible related sources for the name `Whitewall'; the wall round this factory was always painted white, opposite the cottages was a chalk cliff which appeared like a lofty wall, and the lane that once went down from Manor Farm to the river was called Whitewall Road because of the abundance of chalk. Nearby was a smaller creek known as Gallery Creek, or locally as Convict Creek. Here in the time of Dickens the bodies of prisoners from the many hulks moored in the Medway were brought ashore to be buried at Upnor, and `Conwict' (sic) Creek appears in `Great Expectations'. Whitewall Creek, however it may have acquired its name, occupies a part of the Medway Towns called `Frindsbury Extra', which, as the last word suggests, lies outside the City.

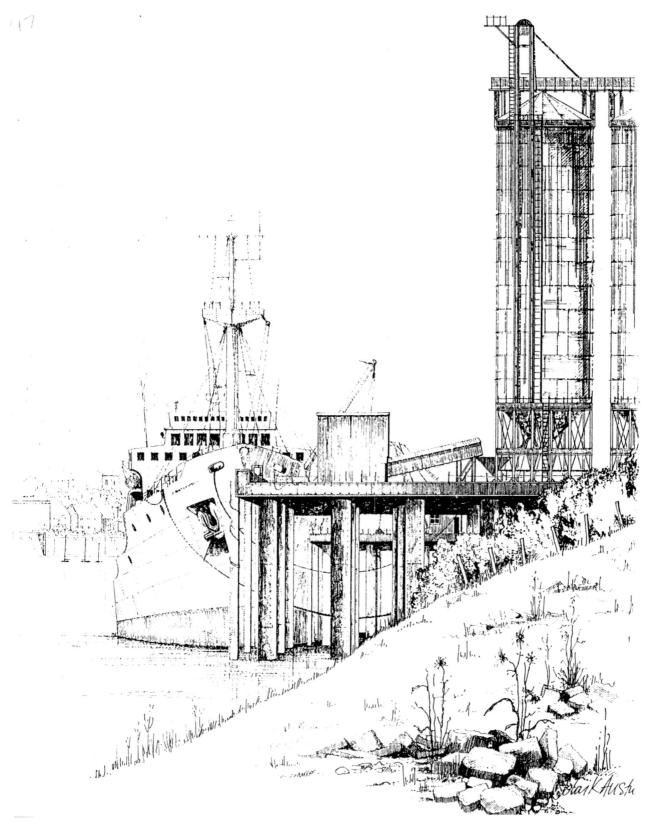

Neptune Wharf, Chatham Ness

Several of the barges left to rot in the creek at the end of the War took on a new lease of life as houseboats, either by choice or possibly because of the acute housing shortage. Surplus barges, because of their numbers, could be purchased quite cheaply, especially if they had just been released from war service. During their time with the government very little, if anything, had been done in the way of deck dressing and side cleaning, essential in keeping the weather out. For a time at least such vessels became, after conversion, quite spacious and comfortable detached homes, each with its own anchorage and rickety wooden pier. Dressed overall on washdays they added a splash of colour to an otherwise sombre landscape, and brought life back to Whitewall Creek.

The hulked Barge 'Bedford' at Whitewall Creek

A fellow student, a Polish refugee and a fine modern painter, lived aboard one of these barges. Several of us used to visit him quite often to sit well into the night discussing the things that matter to students. Compared with the many dingy bedsitters rented by other students, his houseboat was like a spacious liner. The saloon, once the main hold, made an ideal studio

Remains of S.B. Lord Churchill at Whitewall Creek, Frindsbury

My first encounter with Whitewall Creek, however, was when I joined Skipper Tom Dennis aboard the *Greta* as Third Mate for the first time. We cycled from Rainham early one morning, arriving at the lower end of the creek via the footpath which led to Frindsbury over the old canal lock gates near Strood Pier. The Second Mate was already aboard, with the kettle on and the tea brewing. But instead of taking in the view I was allotted the task of scraping a black-treacle gunge from the bottom of the hold. Tom explained that they had taken a parcel (cargo) of oil in drums from Berry Wiggins at Hoo, and a couple of drums had split open.

Apparently Whitewall Creek was well-used by skippers who needed a temporary dry dock to carry out the odd repair, or to do some painting and scraping between jobs. Over the past few years this bit of sadly-neglected marshland between Strood and Upper Upnor has undergone a complete facelift under the local land reclamation scheme. Where once only seabirds nested fresh river wharves have been excavated opposite the Ropery end of the old Naval Dockyard. A wide main road leads to Chatham Ness and others branch from it to new brick factory buildings and warehouses. This reborn part of the Medway Towns is called `Medway City Estates', and is emerging from the gloom of unemployment which followed the closure of the Dockyard in 1984.

As for the *Lord Churchill,* she has disappeared without trace. A few years ago the local paper reported that an old barge from Whitewall Creek had broken her moorings and drifted out into Chatham Reach. Was this the famous *Lord Churchill?* Perhaps somebody knows. In more recent times another houseboat, the *Brownie,* has taken up residence at the very top of the creek near the road to Upnor. According to A.S. Bennett's `Us Bargemen' the *Brownie* was one of only a handful of barges still in sail to be retained after the War by the London and Rochester Trading Company. When I last visited what is left of the old creek she was still there and, judging by the washing on the line, still inhabited. But no-one answered my knock.

UPNOR CASTLE AND THE DUTCH IN THE MEDWAY

The village of Upnor, originally recorded as `Upnore' meaning `upon a bank', sprang up in association with the castle. Its name is sometimes preceded with the word `Upper' to ease the. confusion between this village, the quieter of the two, with Lower Upnor, of *Arethusa* fame, which lies about a mile downstream. Upper Upnor has a little main street of mainly weather-boarded cottages and houses, all extremely well-loved and cared for, and boasts two public houses, `The King's Arms' and `The Tudor Rose'. The miniature Post Office still advertises `Daren Bread'. This little High Street actually ends at the entrance to the castle, where what is left of the old Dockyard is seen opposite, across the short stretch of Medway water known as Upnor Reach.

High Street, Upper Upnor

Upnor Castle was built as a result of the Tudor Dockyard becoming bigger and spreading downstream from its original Gun Wharf site, below St Mary's Church. The Castle was erected on the orders of Queen Elizabeth I, in the third year of her reign. Richard Watts of Rochester (Watts Charity) was appointed as Paymaster, Purveyor and Clerk of the Works. The stone for the building of this important bulwark was to be taken from Rochester Castle, though whether it was or not nobody really knows.

On Wednesday 12th June 1667 a Dutch fleet of about seventy ships, having taken Sheerness Fort, sailed up the Medway to fire and plunder His Majesty's ships anchored in `Jillingham Water'. The defensive chain weighing twelve tons which stretched from Hoo Ness to Gillingham proved little more than a minor obstacle to Rear Admiral Vling. It was strongly believed that some of the Dutch seamen were renegade Englishmen, who had probably worked at Chatham Dockyard, where the men's wages were sadly very much in arrears. Their dissatisfaction had led them to revenge and their knowledge of the whereabouts of the chain made this line of defence utterly useless. The securing bolt was long preserved at Enkhuisen in Holland as a trophy of the invasion.

The low state of the tide on the night in question prevented the Dutch advance up the river to Chatham, allowing the English defenders commanded by the Duke of Albemarle time to surround the town with a force of 6,000 men, and to set up a battery of eight guns on the north side of the Dockyard. In addition three ships *(Royal Catherine, St George* and *Victory*) were sunk in the main passage of the Medway to hinder the enemy's progress.

About mid-day next day seven Dutch frigates and sloops sailed up the river to attack the English ships. Two of the enemy anchored before Upnor Castle and opened fire. Major Scott and his men returned their cannonade, as did the temporary batteries from the Dockyard opposite. In the meantime Sir Edward Spragge, having escaped from the doomed fort at Sheerness, set up another battery in Crockham Wood about a mile downstream from Upnor Castle on the Hoo bank. Had the Dutch pressed their attack with greater vigour the Dockyard and every ship would have been destroyed and Upnor Castle reduced to a ruin. But the Dutch, having destroyed six vessels and captured the English flagship, the *Royal Charles,* seemed content with their success and retired to Queenborough, remaining at anchor for several days before departing our shores for good.

Lower Upnor

22

As a result of this attack a belated Royal Warrant was issued in July of the same year ordering that Upnor was `henceforth to be kept up as a fort and place of strength'. The following year it was decided to convert the castle into a gunpowder magazine

Upnor Castle

.The extent and overall layout of the castle, and its guardianship of the Royal Dockyard opposite, cannot be appreciated from the illustration, which shows only the South Tower. There are in fact five such towers, all facing towards the river. The castle, especially when seen from the air, looks every bit like a child's toy fort.

During the Second World War the castle was damaged when two bombs fell in an adjacent garden demolishing a bungalow. Luckily the fortress escaped being seriously scarred, and it stands today as a reminder of the river's turbulent past.

GILLINGHAM PIER, HOO ISLAND AND THE ESTUARY

The final stretch of the southern Medway shore between Gillingham and Otterham Quay stretches almost four miles as the crow flies. Gillingham Pier, referred to in a sepia postcard as `The Harbour', is now little known compared to the Gasworks and the Strand. The two old jetties, with the cobblestoned hard between them sloping towards the incoming tide, were originally built by the Admiralty in the late 1860s. The cost, staggering in those days, was some £330,000. The pier was given to the people of Gillingham to replace the old Gillingham Bridge Wharf and Collier Dock, situated off St Mary's Creek near St Mary's Island. The Admiralty had taken the latter area for the extension of the Dockyard; St Mary's Creek formed part of one of the three new basins completed towards the end of 1885. The `Bridge House' hostelry in Medway Road near the old Gillingham Gate is said to be not far from the site of the bridge which once crossed the creek.

In his `History of Gillingham', published in 1922, Harris states that `Lower Gillingham is mostly inhabited by persons belonging to the Dockyard and other departments of government'. Today I suspect that few fall into this category. But normal life goes on in and around the narrow streets of neat terraced dwellings which extend down to Pier Road, though some of the little corner shops have succumbed since the closure of the Dockyard a decade ago.

The finished pier was formally opened on 13th February 1873. The first ship to use it was the *Hannah,* a brig belonging to Mr Filmer, a local coal merchant. Three months later, on Good Friday, 11th April, pleasure boats belonging to the Medway Steam Packet Company called at Gillingham Pier for the first time, and records show that four hundred passengers used the pier on that day. Soon silting-up of the river at the pier caused problems, so that not many years after its completion, plans were drawn up for a replacement pier to be built at Commodore Hard (The Strand). Apparently nothing came of this idea.

To the casual onlooker the western arm of the pier (once called Crane Wharf because of its travelling crane), and the hard area next to it, look a bit run down. But to the frequent visitor the scene looks as it always has, with small boats under repair, a Thames lighter moored, boys fishing with rod and line from the very end of the pier: not a lot happens. Occasionally, along the quay built of bricks fashioned by convict labour on St Mary's Island, a freighter is seen berthing: I watched the *Anita-C,* Rochester-registered, tying up. I often wander down to my favourite little tea-bar here.

The pier retains the sounds and smells of a live harbour, with lots of little boats like the *Maggie-May, Julie-Sue* and *Little Daisy.* Countless others are berthed, shackled to the tyre-festooned, once sturdy, uprights that line each side of the central hard like tired sentries. Many of the boats never seem to move except when stirred by the tide as the oily, muddy, river bed fills with water. The stillness of the pier is broken only at weekends when it bursts into life as paintpots are prised open and toolboxes searched as part of the boat owners' weekly ritual. Some of the boats even manage to splutter into life and venture out on the ebb, but others just sink deeper into the mud, shedding a little more paint from those parts not camouflaged by torn and faded sheets of tarpaulin.

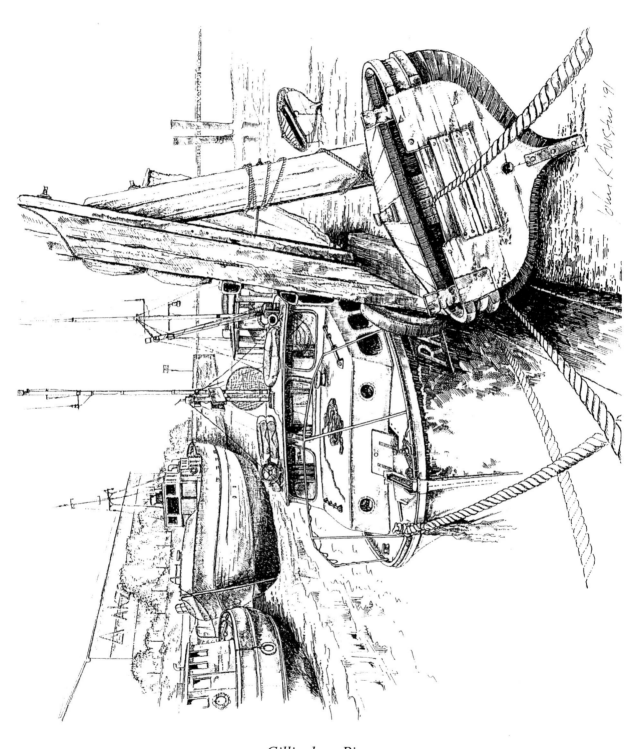

Gillingham Pier

The eastern arm is a complete contrast. Still affectionately called `Admiralty Pier', the extreme end was for many years used by the naval trot-boat service when lines of warships were anchored down the estuary. The same pier is still very much in demand by passing boats for diesel, water and other marine services available there seven days a week. The whole area is in the care of the Gillingham Pier Association, which took over its management from the Borough Council.

In duffel coat, scarf and cap I sat huddled against a biting January breeze to make the drawing showing the special character of the Pier Master's office. Perched on the end of the eastern arm, it was built about 1914, and would not look out of place in some quaint Cornish harbour. It adds the finishing touch to a lovely bit of Gillingham waterfront. Sadly the approach is less hospitable. Several ugly signs declaring that the pier is not for general use deny access to what, after all, was given to the people of Gillingham.

Gillingham Marina, which lies immediately down-river, occupies most of the river frontage from the pier to the Gasworks. Old maps indicate that this section of the river went by the name of `Herry-Hang Wharf, with curing sheds nearby. Part of the same area was more recently called Bennett's Wharf. As at Strood, fishing at Gillingham during the last century was not a pastime but a way of life. It was governed by the Admiralty Court, which put Gillingham Reach out of bounds to dredging because of pollution by the Navy's activities, and by sewage. But difficulty in making a living meant that the ban was more often than not `forgotten'. Recently the marina was granted a `Five Gold Anchors' award by the Yacht Harbour Association; a much coveted prize. Facilities at this 500-berth marina even include a helicopter landing pad, and smart luxury cruisers and fibre-glass yachts replace the Gillingham fishing fleet of yesterday.

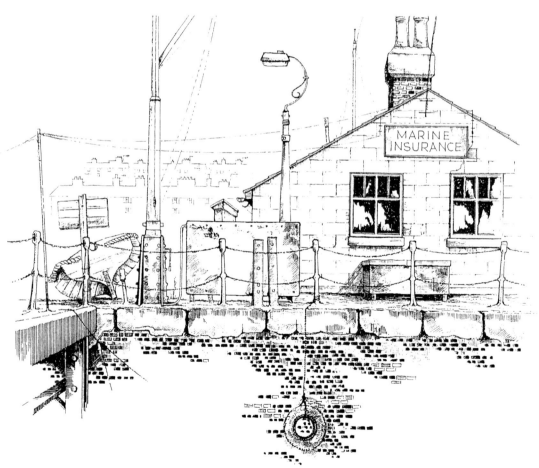

The Piermaster's Office at Gillingham Pier

This same area, much of it marsh in the mid-nineteenth century, was known as 'Prisoners' Bank', for an estimated 1,700 French prisoners-of-war were interred here. By 1869 the last of their remains had been removed and re-interred at St Mary's Island, where they were recently rediscovered by contractors developing that area for housing.

From its source in leafy Sussex, through Kent to Gillingham Pier, the Medway is quite narrow, and its snaking route is easy to follow. At Gillingham Reach, however, the river becomes much wider. Its uninhabited islands and saltings are intersected by creeks whose waters recede at low tide to expose extensive mudflats. The north bank of the reach is formed naturally by Hoo Island, the desolate marshy terrain of Hoo Ness being visible from the end of Gillingham Pier. At the island's most easterly point is Hoo Fort, also known as Folly Point. This squat round fort was one of two river bulwarks built in 1861, each armed with a 12.5 ton gun in 1874, though these were never used. Darnet Fort faces its counterpart from the end of Pinup Reach just over half a mile away.

During the reign of Charles I a third fort was built on saltings near St Mary's Island. Gillingham Castle, as it was sometimes called, was not completed until after the Dutch raid. According to Edwin Harris only four guns could be used at the time of the invasion, though the accuracy of this statement is somewhat doubtful. Nothing remains of it today, for it was demolished after falling into disrepair during the eighteenth century.

The railway viaduct at the junction with Pier Approach Road is another link with the past: This dockyard line was established over a hundred years ago in 1877, when much of the area was described as 'marshy and extremely unhealthy'.

Small craft at Gillingham Pier

THE STRAND AND GILLINGHAM CREEK

The Strand (called `The Riverside Lido' in the 1938 Borough guide) was first opened in June 1896 on a strip of river frontage referred to as `Gillingham Hard'. This same strip was also known as `The Causeway' and as `Commodore Hard'. Initially it had the name of `Cuckow's Public Seawater Swimming Bath'. Long before the other attractions associated with the present-day Strand were added the area was a popular local seaside venue. The aroma escaping from the Gasworks next door did not stop our youthful fun once the wartime barbed wire and other sea defences were removed from the fringe of the shingle beach, and the boating pond, our favourite pursuit, was returned to peacetime use.   Surprisingly enough Mr Cuckow was not the first person to create a swimming bath in the area, for in 1838 an attempt was made to promote Gillingham as a spa, and to hail the saline properties of its water. An establishment at that time offered `separate bathing rooms' at a floating bath moored near Gillingham Fort.

Just across the road from the Strand, on the higher ground overlooking the river, there used to be the training ship *Cornwallis*. This was in fact an old community hall of red brick, which was used for many years as the Headquarters of the Medway Towns Sea Cadets. Redevelopment has eroded all trace of it. Run like a ship, the *Cornwallis* had a muster deck and officers' mess as well as everybody's favourite, the NAAFI. The original *Cornwallis*, I found out only recently, was a 74-gun ship built in Bombay in 1816. It was used for a time as a pier in Sheerness Dockyard.

Gillingham Gasworks

Waterside Lane, Gillingham

Beyond the Strand, with its swimming pool, boating lake and miniature railway, the footpath crosses the shingled moorings of the Medway Cruising Club, founded in 1895, before passing in front of three small cottages standing only feet away from the river's edge. Situated opposite the mudflats called `The Ovens' at the bottom of Gillingham Creek, numbers 65, 67 and 69 Waterside Lane must be the three most exposed dwellings along the whole length of the Medway. These three are all that now remain of a whole row of two-up, two-down cottages that have faced high tides, winds and rain for over two hundred years. A map in Gillingham Library dated 1898 shows only these three, the others having presumably been swallowed up by the cement works. Recently I spent an hour at No. 69, `The Moorings', chatting to its owner. `Built around 1770-80', he told me, `long before the cement works was erected.' All three cottages retain several of their original Georgian features: peg-tile roofs, stout outer walls, sash windows, and homely brick fireplaces inside. Although all have been extended and improved they have not lost that special charm that belongs to cottages of this particular vintage.

From the Strand it is easy and very pleasant to walk along the riverbank almost without interruption to Otterham Quay. The original route was carved out long ago by the Romans and Saxons, and today this coastal track, which extends from Gravesend to Rye in Sussex, is known and signposted as the `Saxon Shore Way'.

My next drawing illustrates the dock area of the old cement works, previously the site of a well-known shipyard which was primarily concerned with Admiralty work and the repair of ships. The yard was started by David Duck, a dockyard officer, and passed to the Pett family in 1604. The Muddle family, by whose name the yard is best remembered, took control from about 1680. When Admiralty work ceased about 1808 it is thought that the yard continued by building smaller boats, like those used by the Medway fishermen. Muddles Yard was quite definitely in existence when all the cottages along Waterside Lane were built. It is likely that several were occupied by those employed in the yard, especially shipwrights, who often lived almost next door to their place of work.

The Kent Post Office Directory for 1874 records for the first time the `Gillingham Portland Cement Company Limited' at Danes Hill. J.M. Preston, in his `Industrial Medway', states that it was founded by George Burge in association with accountant William Morgan and civil engineer C.R. Cheffin, who owned Grange Manor. Works manager Burge appears to have been connected with several of the cement works in the Frindsbury area in the 1880s as well as with the Falcon Works at Otterham Quay in Rainham which he set up with Frederick Barron in 1882.

During the cement depression of the 1890s the Gillingham company was taken over by J.B. White, owner of the Bridge and Globe Works at Strood, but it closed about 1911. There was a revival in 1920, and ten years later a 200-foot rotary kiln was installed. Fortunes fluctuated throughout the thirties, and the works belonged for short periods to the Cement Makers' Federation and to the Amalgamated Roadstone Company before a final sale to the Rugby Portland Cement Company in 1939 at a price of £130,000. Closure followed within a few months and the site was sold, though the very tall solitary chimney which had replaced the site's many smaller ones survived until well after the war. During the war the area was used by the Admiralty for submarine repairs.

Some of the original cement-encrusted architecture has survived, including a gabled wall of brick bearing the name `Gillingham Portland Cement Co.', two large squat circular kiln-type buildings, and the quayside shown in the illustration. New buildings have sprung up to accommodate the needs of the firms now in occupation at the old riverside site.

The roadway at the side of the site, called Owens Way, was once the main tramway route from the chalk quarry, now the corporation refuse tip near Woodlands Road. The 1898 map referred to earlier shows a mini-Clapham Junction of tramway lines behind the buildings featured in the drawing.

Along the switchback road through Gads Hill and Danes Hill many of the buildings, with their front doors opening onto the pavement, belong to the older Gillingham dominated by the parish church of St Mary's only a stone's throw away. Here we leave the urban area behind as, at the bottom of Danes Hill, we reach the hostelry known as the `Hastings Arms'.

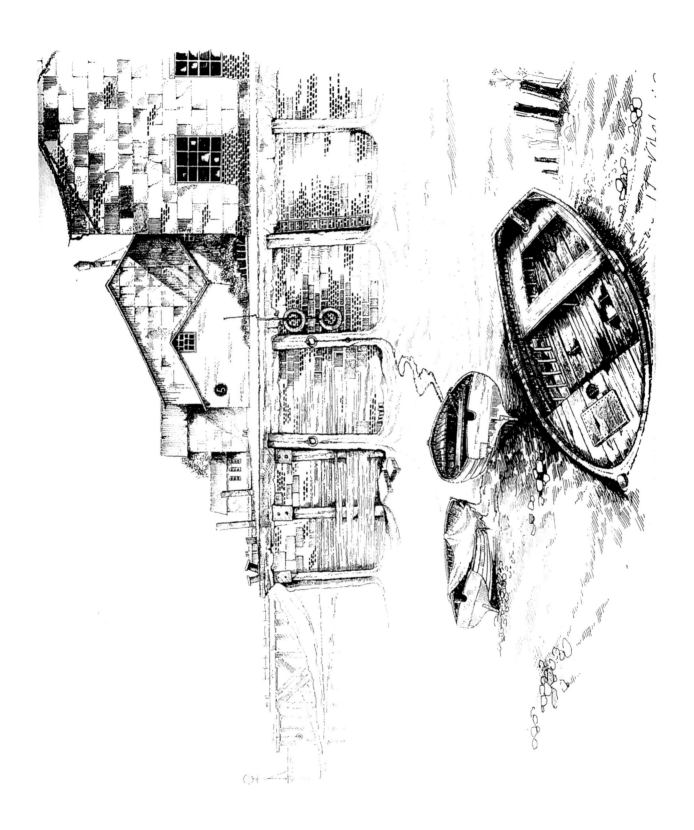

The Medway at Gillingham Cement Works

CINQUE PORT MARSHES, GRANGE MANOR AND THE COPPERAS INDUSTRY

The Saxon Shore Way is diverted round the last remaining buildings of the old cement works via a muddy path which skirts the newer factory premises at the end of Owen's Way. The twisting footpath penetrates deep into a copse of ivy-covered bushes, sadly blotted with scattered household rubbish spilling from plastic sacks. A blackbird disturbed by my trespass into his kingdom eyed me suspiciously before swooping away. The path ends abruptly, revealing as it does so the expanse of the Cinque Port Marshes. In the distance the saltings of Copperhouse Marshes become visible as the eye begins to take in the breadth of the estuary's sweeping watercourse.

The causeway stretching back to what remains of the cement works to the left, once criss-crossed with tramways, forms the western side of the Cinque Port bay. At low tide the giant Kingsnorth power station on the Hoo side of the estuary and Hoo Fort in midstream are seen as though both landmarks are joined to the mudflats of Gillingham Creek. Glancing inland from this point I could see the 'Hastings Arms', and, on higher ground directly above the hostelry, the impressive black and white gables of Grange Manor.

The ancient manor of Grange was called in mediaeval times 'Grench', the name signifying a farm with a house. Since the thirteenth century Grange, a limb of the Cinque Ports, has had the responsibility of providing two men with two oars to serve with the ships of Hastings - hence the name of the public house and the surrounding marshes. Records show that the Mayor of Hastings last visited Grange to beat the bounds of this particular Cinque Port in October 1873.

The present house, standing at the end of a sweeping drive, dates from the mid-eighteenth century, although the stone porch is apparently of a different period from the overall facade of this lovely building. The house, now a retirement home, displays an almost forgotten elegance, each aspect being in perfect balance with every other part. The superb proportions extend to outbuildings like the chauffeur's lodge, which was once the stables and coach-house. The hay-loft door is still intact.

When I used to deliver groceries to this very house over thirty years ago I got to know the housekeeper quite well. She was a dear old soul in her sixties, with silver hair done in a bun, and she always wore a crisp starched apron. One day I was in her kitchen having a cup of tea as usual when, like a character from a Jane Austen novel, the lady of the house walked in and enquired who I was. Doffing my cap, I retreated hastily with the empty boxes. Thereafter I had my tea on the back doorstep.

In the grounds are the remnants of two mediaeval buildings, both roofless. One is believed to be the remains of the chapel already in existence when Sir John Philipot, Lord Mayor of London in 1397, acquired the Manor, and which he decorated with his coat of arms. The other, which is in a less ruinous state, resembles an old barn and is situated nearer the road opposite Short Lane.

Grench Manor

Not far from the Grange, opposite what was once the little public house called the `Mulberry' (whose name is still visible above what used to be the saloon bar), is a muddy track called Copperhouse Lane. A creek called Copper House Creek once existed somewhere near this spot. During the eighteenth century the creek was used by local people engaged in the copperas industry. Copperas, used to make a dye for the woollen and textile trade, was obtained by allowing stones containing iron pyrites (sometimes called `Fool's Gold') collected from the beach at low tide to ripen in special reservoirs for up to six years. The resulting liquor was drawn off and boiled over a furnace believed to have been sited somewhere in the area around the `Mulberry Tree'. Evaporation produced copperas crystals, which were carefully taken off and either used locally or transported by river to London. A map in Gillingham Library dated 1742 shows copperas beds and a cluster of buildings, possibly the copperas works, in the vicinity of Grange and Sharp's Green.

The area around the `Mulberry Tree' is known as Mill Hill, the name presumably coming from the windmill named Friday's Mill which once stood at Mill Hill Farm. The 1897 Ordnance Survey map shows the mill as `disused', while another source of information says that it was demolished in 1896.

A postcard view of the public house taken about 1900 shows a group of thirsty cloth-capped and bowler-hatted regulars outside the Style and Winch alehouse. Next door was a single-fronted grocer's shop. Now both are private dwellings, part of a homely terrace of two-storey cottages named and dated `Mulberry Tree Place 1858'. My drawing illustrates one end of the terrace today.

Mulberry Tree Place

EASTCOURT MEADOWS, SHARP'S GREEN AND RIVERSIDE COUNTRY PARK

One damp and foggy December afternoon, unable to sketch because of the poor visibility, I decided instead to walk the short distance along the Saxon Shore Way between Copperhouse Marshes and the Riverside Country Park at Sharp's Green. The sea wall at the eastern end of the Cinque Port Marshes at the bottom of Copperhouse Lane is quite high, with a gully on the landward side protecting allotments and a small paddock from any river overspill. The pathway, which follows the sea wall, was narrow and very muddy here. Bangs, clatterings and gushes of steam coming from across the river sounded especially eerie, as their source, Kingsnorth Power Station, which normally dominates the estuary, was shrouded in fog. More booms from the same area reminded me of the passage in `Great Expectations' where the sound of cannon fire across the marshes prompted young Pip to ask `Was that great guns, Joe?'

Beyond the former Matthews' riding school the narrow path becomes wider, eventually opening out into the western end of the recently created country park. Here, where trees, grasses and scrub grow on what was once a refuse tip, is to be found the `long leaf', a plant which grows in just two other parts of the country. The beach along this stretch of river is still defended as it was fifty years ago by concrete blocks to slow up any invading army. Along this same stretch two hundred years earlier local people collected stones for the copperas industry.

Remains of Cement Works, Horrid Hill

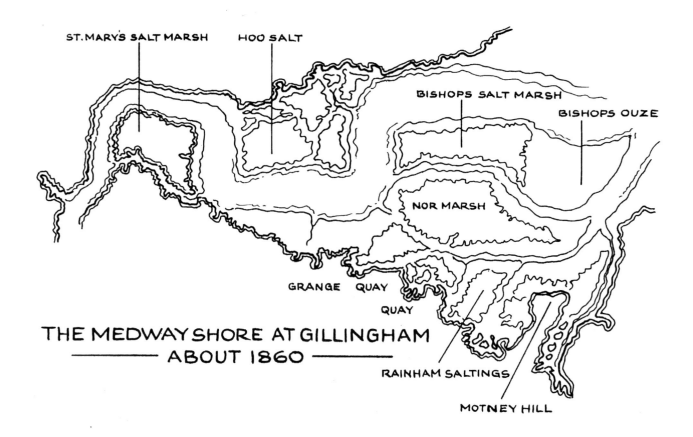

ST. MARY'S SALT MARSH   HOO SALT

BISHOPS SALT MARSH

BISHOPS OUZE

NOR MARSH

GRANGE QUAY

QUAY

THE MEDWAY SHORE AT GILLINGHAM
———— ABOUT 1860 ————

RAINHAM SALTINGS

MOTNEY HILL

Small boats of all types and in all states of seaworthiness became gradually visible as I stumbled towards the shingle beach, adjacent to a smooth concrete causeway leading to the peninsula known as Horrid Hill. Little now remains on this spit of land of one of the river's smallest cement works, the `Sharp's Green Cement Company Ltd'. It was erected in 1902, built from second-hand machinery, and was one of the last works on the Medway to use static chamber kilns. Chalk was supplied by Alfred Castle from the Twydall Quarry, and was carried to the works along a wagon way which crossed the Lower Rainham Road before trundling down the causeway to Horrid Hill. The company closed in 1913, and in 1940 the rails were torn up when scrap metal was being sought for the war effort.

The beach is still littered with fragments of `Dundee Orange Marmalade' jars, no doubt coming from the Keiller pottery works at Faversham. It is quite feasible that these jars, many of which were still whole when I played on the beach as a boy, were part of the cargo of the sailing barge *Dick Turpin,* built at Otterham Quay in 1870. She went aground in the bay in 1913, and was reputed to have been the last vessel to be berthed at the old Sharp's Green Quay. In the days of sailing barges these jars were always used by the crews as tea mugs.

It has been suggested that smuggling went on round these estuary shores, with secluded places like Sharp's Green seeing numerous illicit cargoes brought ashore. On an evening such as this, with fog providing the perfect cover, it was not difficult to imagine the scene. Evidence dated 1725 at the Kent Records Office shows that Otterham Quay was another spot favoured by smugglers.

As part of the Riverside Park this short stretch of the Medway riverbank seems safe from any harmful development. Its pond is an important breeding site for newts, and its marshes and reed-covered mudflats provide nesting and feeding areas for many varieties of birds. The park is well worth a visit, and its Rangers are always ready to answer questions about the area and its wildlife.

Walking back up Sharp's Green Lane to retrieve my car from where I had left it near the old `Mulberry Tree', I was reminded of the little mission church that once stood at the top of the lane. No trace of it remains, apart from the weed-entwined arch of aged wrought iron still linking two squat pillars of crumbling brick just visible among the dense undergrowth. The church was one of three small chapels which once accommodated the various religious needs of this sprawling riverside community. The other two, both in Lower Rainham, will be mentioned in the next section.

Entrance to the Former Mission Church, Sharp's Green

The drawing of Sharp's Green shows a rather dilapidated motor launch on a mudbank in the foreground, with two Thames lighters marooned on another mudbank further out in the estuary. Nore Marsh is seen in the distance on the other side of South Yantlet Creek. Dominating the entire scene is the giant Kingsnorth Power Station, over two miles away on the Hoo shore, the other side of Long Reach. Completing the composition on the left is Darnett Fort, which, with its neighbour Hoo Fort, still guards the narrow approaches to what was Chatham Dockyard. As I sketched, the owner of the launch, which was named *Tecova* (`Avocet' spelt backwards), emerged. A keen birdwatcher, he pointed out different waders to me. `That's a female dunlin - they like these muddy shores at low tide. They dig for little worms just below the surface shingle.' This amused me in view of the nearby sign reading `No bait-digging'.

Kingsnorth is Britain's largest dual-fired power station, burning 800 tons of coal per hour and 80,000 tons of oil weekly. Opened in 1975, it can generate a maximum of 2,068 megawatts. The chimney has become a local landmark, being 198 metres (649 feet) high.

Sharp's Green

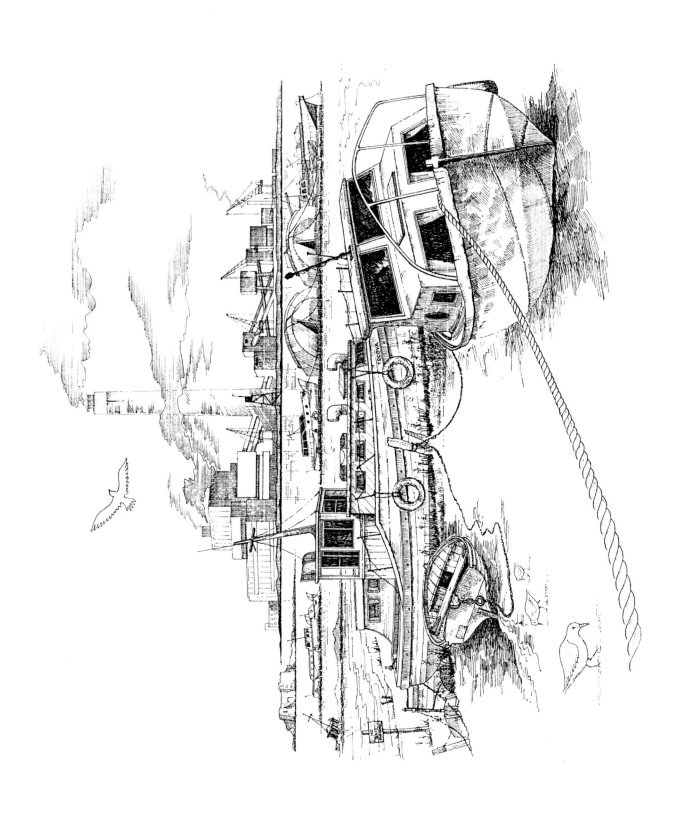

Kingsnorth Power Station seen from Sharp's Green

LOWER RAINHAM, BLOORS WHARF AND RAINHAM DOCK

For most of its route after passing the `Hastings Arms' at the bottom of Danes Hill the main road from Lower Gillingham keeps the estuary in view as it ribbons its way to Otterham Quay. Although never far away the river is lost at times behind houses of varying styles and influences, many named rather than numbered. Most were built between the wars, others are recent additions, but in contrast there are also some much older dwellings.

An example of vernacular architecture, with hipped roof and projecting upper storey, is to be found in Chapel Cottages, at the bottom of Pump Lane. These, sometimes referred to as Chapel House, are believed to form Gillingham's oldest inhabited house, with parts going back as far as the fourteenth century. In modern times the building has been carefully restored, revealing once again its half-timbered walls with their closely spaced studs and narrow panels. Restoration has also removed the central porch and lowered the main end chimney to its original size. In my schooldays the Wood family, whose two sons went to school with me, lived in one of the two cottages.

River Bank near Bloors Wharf

Corner of Chapel House, Lower Rainham

Three public houses grace the Lower Rainham area: the `Three Mariners', the `Army and Navy' and the `Angel' at the bottom of Station Road, once called White Horse Lane. A fourth, the `Jolly Gardeners', not far from the end of Pump Lane, is now a private house. This was probably the oldest of all the local hostelries. Sir Francis Drake is said to have rested here while on his way to visit his father, the Vicar of Upchurch. Another source of information lists the alehouse used by Drake as the `Three Mariners' almost next door, where Hawkins and Frobisher are also supposed to have stayed. As well as its name the `Three Mariners' has other associations with the estuary, for in its dark damp cellar below are two smugglers' tunnels which lead towards the river. This popular hostelry is said to be haunted by three ghostly children, seen playing leapfrog in an upstairs room by the landlord's wife.

Four public houses may seem a lot for what was a small community even in its heyday. It should be remembered, however, that Lower Rainham was very much a river-dominated area of brickies, muddies and cementers, not forgetting the quarrymen and boys from the Berengrave chalk pit - all very thirsty workers. As is the case in most communities the public houses outnumber the places of worship. Gone without any trace are its two chapels. The Methodist and Wesleyan was almost opposite the lane to Bloors Wharf, while the Providence Chapel was sited just in Motney Hill Road. The latter, sometimes referred to as the `Bible Christian Chapel', was turned into a private house. The exact whereabouts of both are clearly shown on the 1897 Ordnance Survey map.

The old Church of England School was situated on the opposite side of the road midway between the former `Jolly Gardeners' and the `Three Mariners'. Like the chapels it has disappeared now. An interesting entry quoted in the book `Old Rainham' tells that in 1877 a Miss Blundell was appointed as the schoolmistress at £60 per annum. In the same year it was decided that boys over nine should go to the Station Road school. The building remained in use as an infant school until 1932.

Unfortunately there is little pleasure today in trying to stroll through the village, for despite signs asking motorists to drive slowly, few do. Local people continue the tradition of selling their garden produce by advertising what is in season on rustic signs erected in their front gardens: `New pots. Ripe toms. Spring cabs.'. The names on the boards do not seem to have changed since the days when, over forty years ago, a friend and I used to trundle our barrow, a box between two old pram wheels, up from Bloors Wharf loaded with seaweed which we endeavoured to sell to local gardeners at twopence a bucket. The wharf lies almost next door to the old Rainham Dock on the Gillingham side. Listed as Blowers Quay, it appears with two others in a survey of `shipping boats' ordered by Queen Elizabeth I in 1566. Blowers Quay belonged to John Tufton the younger, whose name is particularly associated with Rainham. The other two quays were Hastings Quay and Common Quay, but their exact sites are difficult to place accurately. Common Quay could refer to Rainham Dock, although another possible position is a lesser un-named quay shown on the 1897 Ordnance Survey map midway between Rainham Dock and Motney Hill. Hastings Quay is without doubt associated with Grench Manor, and could have been located nearer to Gillingham, perhaps the other side of Sharp's Green.

Blowers Quay naturally takes its name from Bloors Place, a rambling old mansion built at the beginning of the fifteenth century. Today it features a mixture of building styles, including Georgian alterations and Victorian additions. A curious feature of this historic abode of the family of le Bloere or le Blore is the presence of `portholes' in the outer walls, designed as an early warning system against seaborne raiders. Bloors Place is said to be the destination of the headless coachman whom several late-night travellers have reported seeing driving his coach-and-four down Bloors Lane.

The sketches and notes for the drawing showing Motney Hill in the distance across Rainham Creek were made on a very cold December morning, a bitter wind blowing in across the estuary making what is usually a pleasant task into a very bracing encounter with the elements. The coaster *Ahmed Issa* had berthed at Bloors Wharf only a couple of days before. The isolation surrounding the residents of Motney Hill can be appreciated from this drawing.

Rainham Creek & Motney Hill seen from Bloors Wharf

By the end of the Second World War Bloors Wharf had almost disappeared, but a small ship-breaking concern took over the spot very soon afterwards, breaking up small naval ships and landing craft, presumably left over from the D-Day landings. It became a very useful source of timber, not requiring the local council permit needed for the purchase of new wood. The impressive entrance to Bloors Wharf today, with its brick-built reception area, offices and workshops, is a far cry from the post-war muddy entrance strewn with rusty bits of ships and wood ripped from their interiors. Arranged in piles according to length and size, they towered over the little shed with its smoking chimney that served as an office. From here a middle-aged man smoking a pipe would pop out to conjure up a price for a barrow-load of wood. `Half-a-crown that lot, lad, 'cos there's a bit of oak on top,' he would say.

Ship-Breaking at Bloors Wharf

Rainham Dock, Rainham Cement Works

Very little remains of the British Standard Cement Works along Motney Hill Road. These were opened in 1913 by E.J. and W. Goldsmith of Grays, Essex, who were barge owners. In its day the factory was very modern, consisting of two large rotary kilns which were automatically fed with dried slurry. Docking facilities for numerous sailing barges were provided at Rainham Dock next door. My drawing indicates its ruinous state today. Just beyond are the remains of the concrete wharfage bunkers which are virtually all that is left of the once huge cement works which gave employment to a large number of local men until the thirties: during the First World War the places of the absent men were filled by women. In the forties the area was a popular playground in spite of the many warning signs round the works, which were largely intact (though metal parts had been removed for the war effort). The old quarry at the bottom of Berengrave Lane, now a nature reserve, was another favourite place. The terrain was alive with wildlife, especially grass snakes, which some of us kept as pets in our school desks at Orchard Street.

MOTNEY HILL

At the very beginning of this perambulation it will be recalled that I visited the Southern Water Treatment Works at Burham to view and draw the Hawkwood Stone. Now, ten miles or more away and almost at the end of the undertaking to picture and record the Medway shore, I have reached another Southern Water installation, this time the Motney Hill Waste Water Treatment Works.

The sewage works at Motney Hill has significantly affected the development of Rainham, as older residents would agree. This long, narrow spur of land, once an island, was acquired by the Rochester and Chatham Joint Sewage Board in 1923. Had Gillingham, which initially preferred its own main drainage scheme completed in 1899, not joined the Joint Board later, Rainham would quite possibly have developed quietly and independently as a small urban borough. It did, after all, have its own Water Company and Fire Brigade (formed in 1900), and its only connections with Gillingham were the railway link and the bus and tram services. All the sewage from the three Medway Towns gravitated to Motney Hill via a huge underground tunnel network, but Rainham had no such system. In 1907, when the County Council refused to grant urban status to Rainham, it implied that the parish was in need of sanitary improvements. Rainham was at that time part of Milton Rural District, which could not justify the expenditure necessary to provide main drainage in such a remote part of its province. Eventually, on 1st April 1929, the Gillingham Extension Act came into operation, though many Rainham residents objected strongly to becoming a 'suburb' of that town, and refused to include the word 'Gillingham' in their postal address.

.

The first place I wanted to draw at Motney Hill was the old sand dock. Leaving behind some squat round concrete towers I headed north across a wide stretch of freshly mown grass towards the river bank. There, straight ahead and looking bigger than I had imagined, was the end of the dock, bounded by an expanse of tall wild grass and weeds. At its mouth some distance away most of the stout vertical groynes were still in place, but here there were gaps. Like several of the horizontal beams some timbers had disintegrated following years of being pounded by the incoming tide from Bartlett Creek. On the day I saw it in early May the scene reminded me of the Atlantic rollers off the coast of Cornwall, as the wind, whipped up by the incoming tide, produced huge swirling breakers which crashed down on this exposed spot. Through the spray an altogether different view of Kingsnorth Power Station filled the horizon, but the wind, the rain and the spray combined to rule out any idea of a drawing. Instead I cheated and focused my camera!

Medway Estuary at Motney Hill Sand Dock

Hill's Stores, Lower Rainham

Motney Hill, pronounced `Motley' by many local people and written as such on the first ever Ordnance Survey map in 1801, was referred to at one time as `the gritty island', possibly because of its sand. Until the beginning of this century this was still being excavated in quite large quantities and shipped to all parts from the old dock, which is still in existence. Motney Hill separates two small rivers, Rainham Creek on the more exposed west side and Otterham Creek, which leads to Otterham Quay, on the sheltered east. The narrow twisting road to Motney Hill from Lower Rainham starts at the pebble-dashed village shop shown in my sketch. As well as providing for the needs of Lower Rainham's inhabitants, Hill's Stores is also a chandler to ships of all nations.

Retracing my footsteps I took a main footpath which eventually encircled the entire outer boundary of the Waste Water Treatment Works which I was visiting at the invitation of Southern Water. Some of the original buildings and installations, including the pumping station, go back as far as 1923, but the plant was considerably modernised and enlarged during the late sixties in order to cope with the demands of the ever-increasing population of the Medway Towns. On this windswept hill a staggering ten million gallons of domestic waste are treated daily, as well as 30,000 gallons of waste oils. Visitors cannot help but notice how spotlessly clean and tidy the whole site is kept, with neat lawns and colourful borders enhancing its appearance.

Pumping Station, Motney Hill

Stopping to record contrasting buildings in my sketchbook my eye was caught by an ornate well-proportioned facade of warm brick. Surmounted by a little turret, it was reminiscent of the bell tower of a village school, but to my surprise it turned out to be the pumping station, which dates, I believe, from 1923. Unlike the old Chatham pumping station which is now a working museum, Motney Hill still has a job to do almost twenty-four hours a day. In complete contrast are the rather sinister-looking squat circular towers seen in the second drawing. These objects, which initially appear to be guarding the plant from waterborne invaders, remind me of the old Brennan torpedo towers at Cliffe Fort. In fact these huge concrete tanks, with giant pipes forming part of their massive structure, are sewage settling tanks.

Treatment Works, Motney Hill

As I made my way back to the car park where I had left my vehicle a couple of hours earlier the ugly, but at the same time somehow endearing, rusty hulks of abandoned river craft at the end of the creek became conspicuous through the misty rain which had begun to fall. Cold and tired but very satisfied I collapsed into my car and prepared to rejoin the mainland. In the rear view mirror I watched the few houses and small industrial units that make up the Motney Hill community slowly disappear, as the winding road brought me back to Lower Rainham.

From here Otterham Quay, the end of my journey from Burham to Rainham, was only a short distance away. At Otterham no fewer than four natural creeks join the Medway: South Yantlet, Bartlett, Half Acre and finally Otterham Creek itself (sometimes pronounced Otterum). With the exception of Otterham Creek, which is bounded on one side by Motney Hill and on the other by Horsham Marshes, they become a single stretch of water at high tide. As the tide ebbs, however, extensive mudbanks give each creek its own separate identity, creating a maze of muddy channels and inlets stretching to the deeper water at Long Reach.

OTTERHAM QUAY

Otterham, according to Judith Glover's book on the place names of Kent, means `the swollen one', and was originally the water meadow by the swollen stream. The area round this part of the estuary was dominated by water meadows or salt marsh. A former feature of this outer limb of Lower Rainham, referred to as East Rainham in old maps, was sited at the top of Windmill Hill. The windmill, which was burned down in 1916, can be seen in old photographs standing above the `Lord Stanley' public house (now a private house).

In its heyday Otterham Quay was a busy place, with two barge yards. One originated in the 1860s on the east bank, and in 1912 another, Eastwoods, stood at the head of the creek. Close to the earlier barge works at Horsham Marsh, the Falcon Cement Works were started in 1882 by George Burge junior (a name associated with some of the Frindsbury cement works) and Frederick Barron. In his book `Cement, Mud and Muddies' F.G. Wilmott describes these works as fairly large, consisting of `several banks of chamber kilns, a grinding mill, a cooper's shop, and several large wharves that served the works'. The lighter *Harriet* was used to bring the clay from the Motney Hill saltings on the opposite bank. When the saltings were dug away the barge *Snodland* was employed to carry clay from `The Bogs' in Rainham Creek. After being absorbed into the cement combine the works closed in about 1912.

The many brickfields around Otterham Quay, especially those owned by Eastwoods, Wakeley Brothers and the LRTC, added to the prominence of this small community which was separated from neighbouring Lower Rainham in those days by the rows of wooden shutters covering the newly-made bricks. The tiny brickfield reception office along the road fronting the `Three Sisters' still remains, though it is now empty and abandoned. Its size and image are reminiscent of the era of copperplate writing and bosses in bowler hats. One brickfield remains, producing with modern technology but far less labour almost as many bricks as all the original fields put together.

Brickfield Reception Office near Otterham Quay

During its most productive period Otterham had a total of six wharves, according to the 1897 Ordnance Survey map. These would have seen between ten and twenty barges coming and going on each tide, their cargoes including staves for barrel-making, coal, clay, house refuse (`rough stuff) for the brick and cement trade, manure and, occasionally, fish for the farmers of the district. The same barges would depart, often on the next tide, laden with flint, chalk, sand, cement, and new bricks for the ever-expanding Capital. Bricks for the local housing market were transported by horse and wagon.

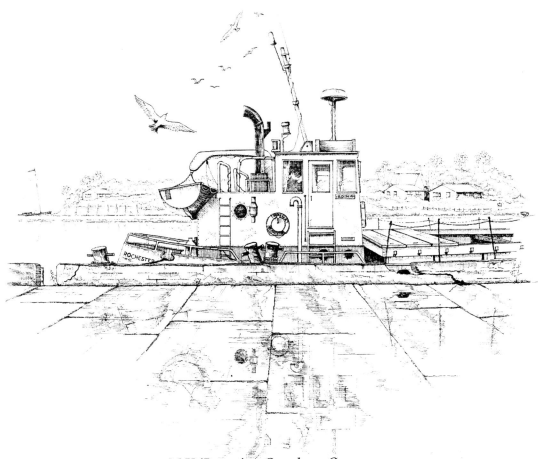

M.V. 'Roina' at Otterham Quay

Needless to say a visit to Otterham Quay today tells a totally different story. At least one vintage Thames lighter and a few old hulks litter the mud of the creek where similar wooden vessels were once constructed by rule of thumb. Very occasionally a freighter may berth at one of the deserted wharves. In place of the barges with their yards of ochre sail, or the brown and orange freighters of Crescent Trading which more recently have used Otterham Quay, containers of a different sort have transformed this once peaceful quay into a huge car park for the modern articulated lorry. Once the grassy bank above the end of the creek was a place for picnics, or for mixing paint or sawing wood. It was here that my love of the perspective and man-made symmetry presented by small boats was created over forty years ago.

A glimmer of the past did appear temporarily during the eighties when Crescent Shipping set up a lifeboat repair and servicing yard. Because of the type of boat and their involvement in rescue missions, boats belonging to the Royal National Lifeboat Institution are often damaged. One important arrival in 1988 was the wartime lifeboat *Jessie Lamb,* built in 1939. To her credit she had a staggering 353 rescue missions to her name. *Jessie Lamb* was repaired and is now on display at the Imperial War Museum at Duxford.

Otterham Quay

The drawing of the boat partly covered by a tarpaulin was sketched early in 1989 before the juggernaut invasion of this estuary beauty spot. Today the extreme end of Otterham Creek is now completely overshadowed by the lorry park literally above it. This sums up what this pilgrimage has been about. How long will it be before the end of this creek too is filled in to make room for more lorries? It should be remembered that Temple Creek, Jane's Creek and Furrells Creek were all once much bigger than the muddy inlets they are today, while gone without trace are Pelican Creek and Common Creek.